Safeguarding Adults

Knowledge and Skills for Social Care Workers series

The Knowledge and Skills for Social Care Workers series features accessible open learning workbooks which tackle a range of key subjects relevant to people working with adults in residential or domiciliary settings. Not just a source of guidance, these workbooks are also designed to meet the requirements of Health and Social Care (Adults) NVQ Level 3, with interactive exercises to develop practice.

other books in the series

Reflecting On and Developing Your Practice
A Workbook for Social Care Workers
Suzan Collins
ISBN 978 1 84310 930 3

Effective Communication
A Workbook for Social Care Workers
Suzan Collins
ISBN 978 1 84310 927 3

Health and Safety
A Workbook for Social Care Workers
Suzan Collins
ISBN 978 1 84310 929 7

Safeguarding Adults

A Workbook for Social Care Workers

Suzan Collins

Jessica Kingsley Publishers
London and Philadelphia

First published in 2009
by Jessica Kingsley Publishers
116 Pentonville Road
London N1 9JB, UK
and
400 Market Street, Suite 400
Philadelphia, PA 19106, USA

www.jkp.com

Library of Congress Cataloging in Publication Data
A CIP catalog record for this book is available from the Library of Congress

British Library Cataloguing in Publication Data
A CIP catalogue record for this book is available from the British Library

Marlow's Hierarchy of Needs, p.17: all reasonable efforts to trace the copyright holder have been made, and any enquiries should be addressed to the publishers.

ISBN 978 1 84310 928 0

Printed and bound in Great Britain by
Printwise (Haverhill) Ltd, Suffolk

Acknowledgements

Lee Nevill (Lowestoft College) for his assistance and support

Simon Kent (Final year student social worker) for his advice and support

David James (Care Quality Commission) for providing data on
Notifiable Incidents

This workbook meets the requirements of the following standards, guidance and qualifications

Care Quality Commission (CQC)
Care Home for Adults Standard 23
Domiciliary Care Standard 14

General Social Care Council (GSCC)
Code of Practice Standard 5

Learning Disability Qualification Induction Award
LDQIA Level 3, Unit 303

National Vocational Qualification in Health and Social Care
NVQ HSC Level 3, Unit 35

Skills for Care (SfC)
Common Induction Standard 5

Contents

Introduction 9

Prevention and Protection 12

Needs and Preferences 17

The Principles of Care 19

Who is a Vulnerable Adult? 25

What is Abuse? 26

Notifiable Incidents 27

Factors that May Make Abuse More Likely to Occur 29

Different Types of Abuse 30

Power 43

Circumstances Where Abuse Can Occur 45

Providing Opportunities to Share Concerns 47

Reporting and Responding to Concerns 48

Barriers to Reporting Concerns 52

Self-harm 54

Questions to Test your Knowledge 58

True and False Exercises 65

Self-Assessment Tool 66

Certificate 67

Knowledge Specification Chart 69

Legislation and Useful Websites 72

References 76

Introduction

As a social care worker you have a responsibility to protect the people you support and working through this workbook will get you thinking about the risks in the service users' lives, how to reduce these risks, how to identify signs and symptoms of abuse and how to report concerns. By identifying the risks early on you will go a long way in protecting the service users from harm and abuse.

You will learn about the different forms of abuse and the signs and symptoms, where abuse can take place and what to do if you have any concerns.

It is not always possible for staff to be taken off the rota to attend a training course and so this workbook has been devised. It uses a variety of training methods:

- reading passages where you will expand your knowledge

- completing exercises

- completing a self-assessment tool which shows you the knowledge you now have

- filling in a certificate which will be completed by the manager or trainer.

As a social care worker, you have to work to certain standards, which are set out by various professional bodies. This workbook links to several standards and if you are not familiar with them, here is a brief explanation of each one.

Learning Disability Qualification Induction Award (LDQ IA) is an induction award that all new staff working with people with learning disabilities must complete within three months of being in post. This workbook meets the communication requirements of the Level 3 award, Unit 303.

Skills for Care (SfC) has a set of standards called Common Induction Standards and all new staff in the care sector (except those who are supporting people with learning disabilities) have to complete these with their manager within three months of being in post. This workbook meets the requirements of Standard 5.

Care Quality Commission (CQC) took over the work of the Commission for Social Care Inspection (CSCI) on 1 April 2009 (it also took over the work of the Healthcare Commission and the Mental Health Act Commission). The CQC has sets of standards for you and your workplace to meet. There are different sets of standards and it will depend on where you work as to which standards you need to work to. If you are unsure please ask your manager. This workbook meets the requirements of Care Homes for Adults Standard 23 (Department of Health 2003) and Domiciliary Care Standard 14 (Department of Health 2000).

Care Homes for Adults Standard 23 (23.14):

> The registered person ensures the provision of training for all staff, including ancillary staff, agency staff and volunteers, in the prevention of abuse, recognition of abuse (including its recognition in non-verbal children), dealing with disclosures or suspicions of abuse, and the home's child protection procedures. This training is included in induction programmes for new staff, including temporary or agency staff, and is ongoing for the staff group in keeping with the aims and objectives of the home.

Domiciliary Care Standard 14 (14.7):

> Training on prevention of abuse is given to all staff within 6 months of employment and is updated every two years.

General Social Care Council (GSCC) has a Code of Practice with six standards in it that reflect good practice. This workbook meets the requirements of Standard 5. Towards the end of the workbook you will be asked to fill in a self-assessment questionnaire on what you have learned from completing this workbook. Once you have done this your Manager or Trainer will complete the certificate and give it back to you.

NVQ HSC is a *National Vocational Qualification in Health and Social Care*.

This workbook has been written first and foremost to protect vulnerable people and prevent them from being harmed or abused and to enable staff to complete 'safeguarding adults' training, without leaving the workplace.

If you are thinking about doing or working towards an NVQ Level 3 in Health and Social Care, you will find that this workbook is a great help to you.

The Health and Social Care Level 3 has four core units and four optional units. This workbook is one of the four core units written to show the knowledge specification. The other three core units are available in this series of books: *Health and Safety, Reflecting on and Developing your Practice* and *Effective Communication*.

When you have registered for an NVQ, you will be allocated an NVQ Assessor who will arrange to observe you in the workplace and guide you through your NVQ award. This guidance will involve devising action plans, which will consist of things like:

- Writing an account of how you did something in the workplace, e.g. helping someone to make a cup of tea, or providing support to enable a service user to follow a training programme, identifying risks, supporting someone to go to the shops etc. This is called a 'self-reflective account' (SRA).

- Asking others to write an account of what you have done. This is called a 'witness report' (WR).

- Completing a set of questions which is called 'the knowledge specification'. This is where you can use this workbook for reference.

This workbook covers all the knowledge specification requirements for the NVQ Unit 35 'Promote choice, well-being and the protection of all individuals', which can be found towards the end of this workbook (see Knowledge Specification Chart).

I hope that you find this a useful workbook and wish you well in your career. This workbook can be:

- read straight through from front to back

- read from front to back, answering the questions as you go, and these can be used as evidence towards the NVQ Unit 35

- used as a reference book.

In this workbook I have referred to the people you support as 'service users' or 'the people you support' or 'he/him' and I have made up two fictitious service users who are called Joe and George.

Name of Learner: . . . .

Signature of Learner: . . . . Date: . . . .

Name of Manager or Trainer: . . . .

Signature of Manager or Trainer: . . . . Date: . . . .

Workplace address or name of organization:

. . . .

. . . .

. . . .

. . . .

Prevention and Protection

We all need activities and goals in our lives and this includes the people you support. Within your role as a social care worker, you will need to know how to support service users to make choices and decisions, identify activities and goals, and play a role in enabling the service users to achieve them. Some service users will achieve this without your help. How much support the service user would like will depend on the individual.

The support plan, which may be accompanied by a risk assessment, will have detailed information on what the service user would like to do or achieve and how the support must be provided and by whom, e.g. yourself, advocate, social services etc. The location of these documents can be in different places: if you work in a residential setting it will be in a locked cabinet and the service user will have his own copy, and if the service user is living in his own home then he will keep it where he wants to keep it. Some may choose not to keep it and you will need to ensure that the office has a copy for you to work from. It is important that you record in the support plan after you have supported the service user.

Within your role you will be privy to a lot of information which is sensitive and confidential. You are being trusted not to tell people unless there is a reason to do so and with the individual's consent.

There are risks attached to almost everything we do, such as crossing the road, going for a night out, getting a bus, going to the bank, having friends, having a relationship, and this is no different for the people you support. If we did not take risks then we would not learn and develop and our opportunities would be limited.

Everyone has a right to choose what they want to do, where to go or what to wear, and some of the people you support may be able to make choices but may not be able to understand that there may be risks attached to their choices. Your role is to enable the people you support to understand this. This does not mean that if there is a risk then the choice does not happen.

If there is a risk you can discuss this with the service user and your manager. The service user and your manager may wish to invite others along to discuss it as well e.g. relatives, social worker, advocate. The meeting can assess the likelihood of the risk, who might be at risk and ways to reduce these risks. All of this will be recorded on a risk assessment form.

In the past the people you support may have been prevented from doing things because of the potential risks attached to them. Some staff think that a risk assessment stops an activity happening and this is incorrect. By completing a risk assessment questions are raised and by answering these it enables the potential risks to be discussed and measures put in place to reduce the risks. *Prevention of harm and abuse is the key phrase!*

A risk assessment should be seen as a tool to enable experience rather than prevent an activity.

✎ Take some time here to think about the ways in which your organization protects the people you support?

. . . .

. . . .

. . . .

. . . .

Did your answers cover any of these?

- All potential employees applying for posts to provide care and support must have an enhanced Criminal Records Bureau (CRB) check. This is called a 'disclosure' check and this will involve checking the police computer to see if a person has a criminal record.

- All potential employees must also have satisfactory references before starting to work with vulnerable people.

- The Department of Health introduced the Protection of Vulnerable Adults (PoVA) guidance which came into force in July 2004. This means that prior to starting in the care field, managers will check to see if the person is included in the PoVA list. If their name is on the list then the person cannot work in the post, as the post will involve supporting vulnerable people.

- Carers already in post can be put on the PoVA list if they have harmed or put at risk a vulnerable adult. (If you are on the PoVA list and you feel you should not be, you can use the appeals process through the Care Standards Tribunal.)

- When you start work, you will receive induction training which will include many topics e.g.

  ○ 'Safeguarding' adults training to prevent harm and abuse

  ○ Health and Safety training to prevent harm and injury to the service users, yourself and others.

- You will learn that the people you support need to feel safe and be safe. One way of enabling this to happen is to check that all visitors have a right to enter the premises. You can do this by checking their identification and if they do not have any with them, do not let them into the building.

You will also receive training on the *Principles of Social Care*. These principles are: respect, privacy, empowerment, inclusion, individuality, independence, dignity, rights, equal opportunities, partnership and choice. You must provide these principles at all times and you will read about them as you progress through this workbook.

If you are supporting service users who present challenging behaviour, then you should receive training to develop the skills to monitor behaviours and implement strategies that will reduce the behaviours over time. There will also be the following policies which you need to be familiar with and follow if you have any concerns that someone is being harmed or abused:

- local multi-agency 'protection of vulnerable adults' policy

- whistleblowing policy

- health and safety policy.

All staff should receive a minimum of six supervision sessions per year. In these sessions staff training needs are identified and staff can discuss with the supervisor if they have any concerns on poor practice. If you are new in post please discuss with your manager what the arrangements are for your supervision and appraisal.

As you will have read, there are many systems in place, including this workbook, for you to learn the signs and symptoms of abuse and what to do if you suspect harm and or abuse is happening and how to protect the people you support.

The General Social Care Council gives the following *Codes of Practice*:

> As a social care worker, you must uphold public trust and confidence in social care services.

In particular you must not:

- Abuse, neglect or harm service users, carers or colleagues;

- Exploit service users, carers or colleagues in any way;

- Abuse the trust of service users and carers or the access you have to personal information about them or to their property, home or workplace;

- Form inappropriate personal relationships with service users;

- Discriminate unlawfully or unjustifiably against service users, carers or colleagues;

- Condone any unlawful or unjustifiable discrimination by service users, carers or colleagues;

- Put yourself or other people at unnecessary risk; or

- Behave in such a way, in work or outside work, which would call into question your suitability to work in social care services

(General Social Care Council 2002, Standard 5)

Does your organization provide training to enable the people you support to:

Know what harm and abuse is?   Yes/No

Know how to report it?   Yes/No

Know who to report it to?   Yes/No

If you have answered 'No' to any of these, please explain what you will do about it.

. . . .

. . . .

. . . .

. . . .

Is there a compliments and complaints procedure in place? Yes/No

If there is one, can the service users understand it? Yes/No

✍ If you have answered 'No' to any of these, please explain what you will do about it.

. . . .

. . . .

. . . .

. . . .

Needs and Preferences

There are various models that can be used to see if an individual's needs are being met and one that I am going to use is the model of Abraham Maslow's Hierarchy of Needs. This is a theory in psychology that Maslow proposed in his 1943 article, 'A theory of human motivation'. As you can see, it has five levels to it, with the most basic needs at the bottom of the pyramid.

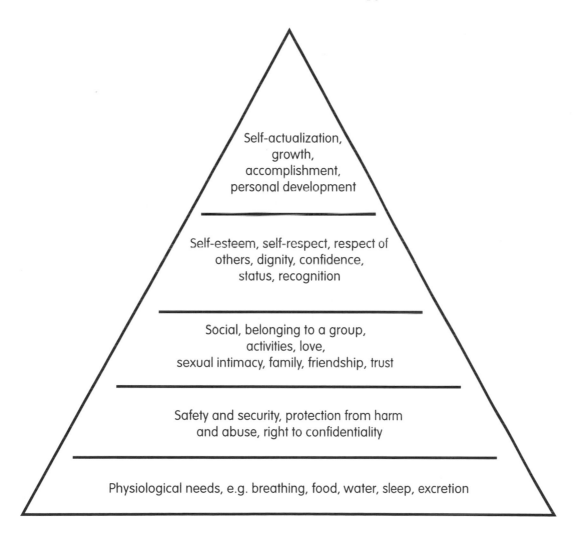

Self-actualization, growth, accomplishment, personal development

Self-esteem, self-respect, respect of others, dignity, confidence, status, recognition

Social, belonging to a group, activities, love, sexual intimacy, family, friendship, trust

Safety and security, protection from harm and abuse, right to confidentiality

Physiological needs, e.g. breathing, food, water, sleep, excretion

✍ Looking at Maslow's Hierarchy of Needs, which levels are being met in your place of work?

. . . .

. . . .

. . . .

. . . .

✍ If the service user has not reached the stages of the hierarchy, how will this affect his or her self-esteem and independence?

. . . .

. . . .

. . . .

. . . .

✍ What can you do to enable the service user to reach all levels? You do not need to do this alone; you can work in partnership with others (e.g. family, friends, circle of support).

. . . .

. . . .

. . . .

. . . .

The Principles of Care

It is important that you provide the principles of care at all times.

RESPECT

You should call the people you support by their preferred name, i.e. the name they choose to use. If someone is a new service user and his records say Mr Terry Smith, do not automatically call him Terry. Ask him what he likes to be called: he may say he likes to be called Mr Smith, and if he does then make a note of this so all staff will call him Mr Smith.

It is important that you listen to what the service user is saying at all times and show regard and courtesy. This will build trust and confidence and raise the individual's self-esteem.

PRIVACY

Everyone has a right to privacy. For example, information you know about the service user must be kept confidential and this will build trust. There will be times when the service user wants to be alone, e.g. listening to music or in the bath or on the toilet.

There needs to be a private area where the service user can receive visitors. Some may like to receive visitors in their bedroom but many might like a different private area and one where others cannot intrude, e.g. a private room. It is important that you or any one else do not listen in on other people's conversations.

It is important that you knock on the door before entering. You must not go into the bedroom if the service user is not in there and has not given you permission to go inside.

EMPOWERMENT

Within your role you will enable the people you support to do as much as they can for themselves. This will provide the people you support with a sense of competence and confidence.

INCLUSION

You will need to enable the service user to be included in activities and making decisions.

INDIVIDUALITY

It is important to see the people you support as individuals with their own strengths, needs, wishes and dreams. Each person will develop a sense of identity and this can be achieved by recognizing the preferences and likes of the person. An example could be supporting the person to decorate his personal space the way he wants to and this will reflect his own taste. Another way is to remember the person's special interest and provide support if required to follow these interests.

INDEPENDENCE

Encouraging the people you support to do things for themselves is very important and you may need to give time for this to be achieved. You may feel that you are doing the service user a favour by doing everything for him but by doing this you will reduce the service user's self-worth and self-esteem and prevent him from progressing, developing or maintaining his current skills.

DIGNITY

It is important to ask service users who they would like to support them with their personal care. The service user's culture may say that it has to be the same sex; female service users may prefer a female to support them. Some organizations have a policy that only same-sex workers will support the service users with their personal care.

Personal care should be carried out discreetly to avoid humiliation and embarrassment.

Promoting dignity is important in how you speak to the people you support. Dignity gives the person self-worth and affords respect.

RIGHTS

With the Human Rights Act 2000 in place we can seek help if we feel that our human rights are being infringed. The Human Rights Act gives us the following rights:

- life
- freedom from slavery, servitude and forced or compulsory labour
- freedom from torture and inhuman or degrading treatment or punishment
- freedom of expression
- right to marry and have a family
- a fair and public trial within a reasonable time

- liberty and security of person

- freedom from retrospective criminal law and no punishment without law

- freedom of thought, conscience and religion

- respect for private and family life, home and correspondence

- freedom of assembly and association

- the prohibition of discrimination in the enjoyment of convention rights

- access to an education

- peaceful enjoyment of possessions and protection of property

- free elections

- not to be subjected to the death penalty.

The people you support have often been denied the right to have the same rights as everyone else. These rights are enshrined in national and international law. You can promote these rights by advocating on behalf of the service user and by challenging any discriminatory practice or behaviour.

EQUAL OPPORTUNITIES

Everyone should have the same opportunities and access to services as everyone else, regardless of age, race, gender, disability, sexuality and culture.

PARTNERSHIP

It is important to work in partnership with the service user and others to achieve aims and goals. By working together you can share responsibilities and decision making and gain views and opinions. This makes the most of resources and values everyone's knowledge and skills.

CHOICE

Service users should choose and express their preferences, e.g. what to eat, what to wear, where to live etc. You need to offer choice, and support the service users to take as much control over their own lives as is possible. Not only does this promote independence but also it raises the person's self-esteem. Not to have choices or to have them stopped suddenly can cause loss of confidence and low self-esteem.

If the service user is able to make choices you will need to enable him to know the consequences of making these choices.

You need to know the person you are supporting and his level of compre-hending, e.g. if he has never been given choice before he could become worried and anxious not knowing what you are asking of him. Also, if he knows what choice is but you have given him too many choices then this could have the same affect. I always become a little worried when I go into a cake shop and I am in a queue: there are too many cakes to choose from and I am very aware of the people waiting behind me. If they only had two cakes for me to choose from I would feel better and would be able to choose from just two items.

VALUES AND BELIEFS

Many of our own values and beliefs come from our past i.e. we learnt these as we grew up and continue to learn them, from friends, work colleagues, TV etc. We may have similar traits to other people and do similar things but we are all individuals with our own values, beliefs and preferences. You will need to be aware that the people you support and the people you work with also have their own values, beliefs and preferences and this makes us all unique.

✍ Case study: a member of staff gives a service user a cup of tea in the afternoon. The service user, who is 65 years of age, says that she does not have a cup of tea in the afternoon; she has a cup of tea mid morning and a cup of coffee mid afternoon, even when she was at home with her mum. The staff member replies that she did not have time to ask her what she wanted and asks that the service user accepts the cup of tea. The service user repeats that she does not have tea in the afternoon and is now getting upset. What are your thoughts on this?

. . . .

. . . .

. . . .

. . . .

✍ Part of your role will be to enable the people you support to have control over their own lives. Think now about two service users and write down four activities that they have had little or no control over. (Some examples could be mealtimes or choice of what to watch on TV.)

1. . . . .

2. . . . .

3. . . . .

4. . . . .

✎ Joe is one of the people you support and he has told you that he would like to go to the shops by himself. What do you now need to do?

. . . .

. . . .

. . . .

. . . .

STRESS

The people you support can feel stressed now and again as we all do. It will depend on what is causing the stress and how the service user is able to cope with it. Some people can cope with stress well, others cannot.

Examples of things that can cause stress:

- not having a choice or being involved in decision making

- living with other people who shout or have the radio on really loud

- having arguments on what to have for tea or what to watch on TV

- dirty dishes being left in the sink.

Whatever the disagreement, you will need to try to resolve it and you can do this by:

- talking in a firm (not raised) voice

- listening to both sides

- reaching a compromise.

✎ If you are feeling stressed please discuss it with your manager or supervisor.

MAKING CHOICES

You may think that the people you support do not understand what choice is or the risks associated with the choices they are making or the question you are asking. You may want to make the decision for the people you are supporting. How will you know if the person you are supporting can make decisions?

The Mental Capacity Act 2005 provides a framework to protect vulnerable people in decision making.

 You may have a copy of the Mental Capacity Act in your workplace. If not you will be able to view a copy on the Internet and you will find the web address in the References of this workbook. It has pages and pages of information. Please have a look at a copy, in particular the following sections:

- Five key principles.

- Independent Mental Capacity Advocate (IMCA).

- The making of 'living wills'.

- The new criminal offence of ill treatment or neglect.

Who is a Vulnerable Adult?

In 1997 The Lord Chancellor's Department defined a vulnerable adult as a person:

> Who is or may be in need of community care services by reason of mental or other disability, age or illness; who is or may be unable to take care of his or herself or unable to protect him or herself against significant exploitation.
>
> (Paragraph 8, 7)

VULNERABILITY

The people you support may be vulnerable to abuse for many reasons. They:

- may need help and support with personal care

- may be dependent on others

- may not know the difference between what is good practice and what is not

- may have communication difficulties and may not be able to get their message across

- may not have been informed that they can complain if they are unhappy with the service

- may not be able to read and/or understand the complaints procedure

- may be unaware of their rights.

They might also be vulnerable because staff have not received training on how to protect vulnerable people from harm and abuse.

Some people's attitudes are that they see people who use services as likely targets because they are vulnerable.

What is Abuse?

Abuse is a violation of an individual's human or civil rights by another person or persons.

(Department of Health and Home Office 2000, para 2.6)

The publication *No Secrets* (Department of Health and Home Office 2000) gives guidance on policy making to protect the people you support.

Abuse is an 'act of commission' when someone does something he should not do. Two examples are forcing the service user to take more medication than he should (overmedicating), and kicking the service user.

When something has been left out on purpose, this is called an 'act of omission'. An example is not giving a service user the prescribed medication.

If the service user does not know what abuse is, how to report it or who to report it to, then the abuse can go unnoticed.

Notifiable Incidents

Within my role as a freelance trainer I deliver training to all groups of people, e.g. service users, social care workers, managers, HR staff etc. When I talk about reporting and who to report to, some service users and social care workers have said that they would like to report to someone outside of the organization but are unsure of who this should be. When I mention CQC they are surprised to hear that they can pick up a telephone or send an email or a letter to CQC raising their concerns.

In August 2008 I approached CQC asking for some data for this workbook and since receiving it I have added the data to my training presentation.

Data as at 28/08/2008	2003/ 2004	2004/ 2005	2005/ 2006	2006/ 2007	2007/ 2008	
Service category	Direct report of abuse/ susp[1]	Direct report of abuse/ susp	Direct report of abuse/ susp	Direct report of abuse/ susp	Direct report of abuse/ susp	Totals
Adult placement scheme			1	1	1	3
Care home with nursing	55	85	63	85	40	328
Home care agency	1	21	12	16	11	61
Nursing agency		1				1
Residential care home	122	135	145	159	87	648
Totals	178	242	221	261	139	1041

1 susp = suspected abuse

Source: David James, CSCI, private email communication, 28 August 2008

Abuse can happen just once or on several occasions.

Q: If it happens only once, should I still report it?

A: Yes!

Q: Why?

A: To prevent it happening again and to protect the people you support.

WHO CAN BE AN ABUSER?

Here are some examples of who can be abusers:

- family
- staff
- carers
- general practitioners (GPs)
- volunteers
- other people in the house or day centre
- friends
- neighbours
- milk delivery person
- taxi drivers.

✍ Can you think of anyone else?

. . . .

. . . .

Abuse can occur in any relationship and may result in significant harm, or exploitation of the person subjected to the abuse. It is not acceptable for abuse to happen in a relationship, with family members or with people who are unknown to the service user.

✍ There may be times when you need to maintain and/or end a relationship with individuals and key people. Please discuss with your manager how you should do this.

Factors that May Make Abuse More Likely to Occur

Here are some examples of factors that may make abuse more likely to occur:

- a desire to exert power over another person
- the abuser might have been a victim of abuse himself
- outdated views
- no clear policies or procedures in place
- a pattern of family violence exists
- staff working in isolation
- drug or alcohol misuse
- relationships placed under stress
- untrained, unsupervised and unsupported staff
- using outdated practices
- low staffing levels over a period of time.

Different Types of Abuse

In this section, you will be reading about different types of abuses and the possible signs and symptoms that can be present. Please be aware that these are possible signs and symptoms of abuse, but they can also be signs and symptoms of something else, e.g. a person you are supporting may have bruises on her hip because she keeps tripping over the carpet. You will need to record everything that concerns you.

This section describes signs and symptoms of the service user. However, be aware that the abuser could also show signs, such as always wanting to be with the service user, or not allowing visitors or telephone calls.

Types of abuse:

- physical
- financial or material
- sexual
- psychological and emotional
- neglect and acts of omission
- self-neglect
- discriminatory
- institutional.

PHYSICAL ABUSE

Physical abuse can include the following:

- punching
- pinching
- slapping
- shaking
- hitting
- sedating
- pushing
- restraining

- scratching

- kicking

- rough handling.

Physical abuse in medication can take the form of undermedicating, overmedicating or withholding medication, and also inappropriately altering medication labels and/or records.

Signs and symptoms of physical abuse can include the following:

- loss of hair in one area and sore scalp

- anxiety or fear

- unexplained injuries

- self-harm

- marks resulting from a slap

- fractures

- sprains

- unexplained burns (e.g. on back of hands)

- drowsiness

- flinching and cowering

- many bruises inconsistent with an explanation (e.g. knocked self, had a fall)

- the service user needs medical advice but will not go to see the GP or frequently changes GPs.

You should not use *control and restraint* unless there is an agreed procedure in place and you have received appropriate training.

Control and restraint should be used only as a last resort. Each time this is used, a control and restraint form must be completed.

 Is control and restraint happening in your workplace?   Yes/No

If you have answered 'Yes', is there an agreed procedure in place?   Yes/No

Have staff received appropriate training?   Yes/No

If control and restraint is happening in your workplace and there is not an agreed procedure in place and/or staff have not received training you must report this immediately.

You can report it to:

- management

- CQC.

✍ A service user tells you that she has bruises on her arms and that the staff did it because she would not do the washing up. What do you do?

....

....

....

....

FINANCIAL OR MATERIAL ABUSE

Financial or material abuse can include the following:

- taking things that belong to the service user

- taking money

- misusing money

- being pressurized to give money away

- being pressurized to change his will

- staff borrowing money from service users

- staff using their own supermarket club cards to get points from the service user's shopping.

Signs and symptoms of financial or material abuse can include the following:

- The next of kin uses informal arrangements regarding the control of finances instead of following advice from the Power of Attorney or the Court of Protection.

- Chequebook has disappeared or individual cheques are missing from the chequebook.

- There is not enough money to pay bills or buy food.

- Possessions go missing.

- Forged signatures are found on financial records.

- Petty cash, service users' monies or their receipts do not tally, or the money is not there.

- Service user buys two for one offer in the shop and the service user has only one of the items.

- Staff buy their own shopping while supporting the service user to buy theirs (thus shopping on the service user's time).

✍ The service user's record of finance shows he bought a DVD on motorbikes. He does not like motorbikes. Write here what you think about this.

. . . .

. . . .

. . . .

. . . .

✍ How can you prevent the people you support being financially abused?

. . . .

. . . .

. . . .

. . . .

Financial abuse can happen if the service user cannot manage his own money. Would any of the people you support like to go to college to learn money skills?

Yes/No

✍ If you have answered 'No', please explain your answer.

. . . .

. . . .

. . . .

. . . .

SEXUAL ABUSE

Sexual abuse can include the following:

- touching of breasts or genitals
- sexual harassment
- rape
- sexual assault
- being forced to look at pornography
- teasing with sexual connotations
- sexual act that the person could not consent to
- taking photographs of a sexual nature without consent
- penetration or attempted penetration of anything in vagina or mouth.

Signs and symptoms of sexual abuse can include the following:

- torn or stained underwear (blood or semen)
- venereal disease
- bruising, pain, bleeding or itching
- pregnancy
- disturbed sleep pattern
- unexplained changes in behaviour
- drug and/or alcohol abuse
- sexualized behaviour.

Rape or a sexual act against the person's wishes when that person is unable to consent is sexual abuse.

✎ George is a heterosexual male and meets up with Colin, who is a gay male, every Tuesday and Thursday evening. George came home tonight and Tuesday night upset. What do you do? Please include in your answer any forms that you need to complete.

. . . .

. . . .

. . . .

. . . .

Would any of the people you support like to have a sexual relationship? Yes/No

✎ If you have answered 'No', please explain your answer.

. . . .

. . . .

. . . .

. . . .

✎ If you have answered 'Yes', please explain what needs to be in place to ensure the safety of the service user.

. . . .

. . . .

. . . .

. . . .

35

PSYCHOLOGICAL AND EMOTIONAL ABUSE

Psychological and emotional abuse can include the following:

- harassing the person

- shouting

- swearing

- not providing stimulation (the amount of stimulation required will be individual to each service user)

- threatening or insulting behaviour

- bullying

- threatening to hurt the person

- holding on to information

- humiliating the person

- not meeting religious or cultural needs

- talking in a different language (making others present feel excluded)

- talking down and devaluing a person, e.g. saying 'You are so stupid!'

Joe lives in sheltered accommodation, on the ground floor. He leaves his lounge window open at night so his son, who is often drunk and homeless, can climb through and sleep there. You are aware this happens. Is this a form of abuse?

Yes/No

✍ What needs to be done to protect Joe?

. . . .

. . . .

. . . .

. . . .

Signs and symptoms of psychological and emotional abuse can include the following:

- disturbed sleep pattern

- aggression or passivity

- talking a lot about one person, e.g. 'I don't like her!'

- unusual weight loss (or gain)

- depression

- withdrawal

- overeating or eating at inappropriate times

- frequently complaining of minor health problems, e.g. tummy ache, headache

- low self-esteem

- fear

- confusion

- running away

- drug and/or alcohol abuse.

Be aware that psychological and emotional abuse may be more difficult to detect.

You have worked on the same shift as another staff member for four days now. You notice that she ignores Joe, who is a wheelchair user. What do you do?

. . . .

. . . .

. . . .

. . . .

NEGLECT AND ACTS OF OMISSION

Neglect is not giving the required care and support that is needed for the individual service user. Neglect includes failing to provide the following:

- privacy and dignity
- nutritional meals
- adequate drinks
- adequate heating, lighting and accommodation
- prescribed medication
- medical, health or care needs
- access to appropriate health or social care or education
- support to use services, e.g. social, health services, police
- support to get to the toilet and use it.

Failure to provide any of the above means you are not protecting the person you support from harm.

Signs and symptoms of neglect and acts of omission can include the following:

- not doing what is needed for the individual
- not doing something that is needed to protect the service user from risk or harm
- incontinence issues not addressed, e.g. odour on clothes, bed, chair
- inadequate clothing
- friends or family not allowed to visit
- unexplained weight loss
- withholding glasses or hearing aid
- unexplained failure to respond to prescribed medication
- repeated falls or slips in the bath not being addressed
- repeated infections
- untreated illness
- encouraging a service user to overeat so it keeps him/her quiet

- no method to call for assistance such as buzzer or call bell

- leaving a service user in the bath (who is not safe to be left alone and there is not a risk assessment in place)

- not supporting a service user to wash, bathe, eat or go out because he/she has challenging behaviour

- staff watching TV and ignoring the service user.

> Neglect is not giving attention and support. It is a legal duty that you do not neglect the people you support. If a service user is harmed, then a court could find you guilty.

SELF-NEGLECT

Everyone has a choice of what they want to do and how they do it (or not as the case may be sometimes). As mentioned early on, some service users may not understand that with choice comes potential risks, e.g. 'I know that if I neglect myself and choose not to wash for a week, no one will want to be by me, talk to me and as a consequence I will feel isolated and lonely.'

> You have a duty to act if the service user's self-neglect becomes harmful.

The people you support could be vulnerable to self-neglect for the following reasons:

- The service user may experience communication difficulties, or may not be able to ask for help.

- Staff may assume that the service user has the skills to do things for himself (e.g. washing, cooking) and he hasn't.

- The service user might not understand the consequences of his self-neglect.

- The service user may have a low expectation of himself.

Signs and symptoms of self-neglect can include the following:

- withdrawal

- not taking medication

- not eating

- not drinking

- not washing self

- staying in bed for days

- not keeping living areas clean and tidy.

✍ Can you think of any more?

. . . .

. . . .

. . . .

. . . .

DISCRIMINATORY ABUSE

Discrimination is to single out a person or a group for special favour or disfavour. Discrimination can be shown on the following grounds: race, age, disability, religion, sexual orientation, colour, culture, ethnic origin.

Signs and symptoms of discriminatory abuse can include the following:

- being withdrawn or isolated

- exhibiting anxiety, fear or anger

- showing lack of respect for or to the individual

- being refused access or being excluded from services

- being excluded from rights given to others, e.g. education, housing, health.

INSTITUTIONAL ABUSE

Institutional abuse can occur when standards and practices fall below an acceptable level. Audits are carried out by the for Care Quality Commission (CQC) against a set of standards.

It is important to know that institutional abuse can happen in both small and large residential, day care or nursing establishments.

Signs and symptoms of institutional abuse can include the following:

- failure to provide choice, privacy or dignity
- staff walking into bedrooms without knocking
- fixed visiting hours
- lack of individual care plans
- not having own bedroom or not having it decorated to choice
- little or no opportunity for the service users to be involved in anything outside of the service
- loss of identity
- an authoritarian regime
- meals being withdrawn as punishment
- poor standards of cleanliness
- always going out in groups
- no phone calls allowed
- no friends or family allowed
- lack of stimulation
- being left on your own for long periods
- no choice
- set mealtimes
- set bedtimes
- inappropriate programmes on TV, e.g. *Andy Pandy*
- smells of urine constantly
- wearing clothes that belong to others.

NB: Some service users need a set routine and others do not. We all need some kind of routine in our lives; however, there needs to be flexibility from time to time. For example, the home always has the evening meal at 5.30p.m. Joe wants to go swimming but staff say he can't because it's teatime. Joe could have his tea later.

✍ Joe does not like faggots and peas and all the staff know this. The staff member on duty tonight says she is going to serve him these because he eats them anyway. What do you do?

. . . .

. . . .

. . . .

. . . .

✍ Why do you think Joe eats the faggots and peas?

. . . .

. . . .

. . . .

. . . .

Power

You can use power in two ways:

- Positively, e.g. to support and empower the people you support to get the services that are required.

- Negatively, e.g. withholding information from the person you are supporting or giving the information using complicated words. For example, an individual sees the GP and explains his problem, and the GP uses complicated words when he tells the individual what is wrong. The individual does not understand what he is saying but will have to accept what the GP has said as being correct; after all, he is the expert! According to French and Raven this is called a negative usage of what is called 'Expert Power'.

In 1960 French and Raven described power in five different forms: Coercive, Reward, Legitimate, Referent and Expert Power. More information can be found at www.changingminds.org/explanations/power/french_and_raven.htm

POWERFUL WORDS

Sometimes words are said without thinking about what they actually mean. Here are a few examples:

'I will *allow* the service user to have a bath before supper.' 'I will *let* the service user have a bath before supper.' This use of the words 'allow' and 'let' implies that the worker is in control.

'*You can* have your bath before supper.' Again, the use of the word 'can' implies that the worker is in control and is giving permission to the service user.

'*Can you* have your bath before supper?' Changing the words around slightly asks the service user a question and puts the service user in control.

Please remember: service users should have the power and control over their own lives and the role of the social care worker is to support, enable and empower the service user to have this power and control.

GIVING POWER TO SERVICE USERS

Give power to the people you support by providing knowledge. Service users need to know how to access information in a format they can understand in the following areas:

- local community, e.g. library, shops, post office, bank
- leisure and education, e.g. sports centres, adult education centres
- media, e.g. talking books, radio, TV, how to use the Internet
- health services, e.g. doctor, hospital, outpatients clinic, dentist
- Citizens Advice Bureau.

Circumstances Where Abuse Can Occur

Abuse can occur in the following circumstances:

- places that we think are safe

- carers going into the person's home

- police stations

- hospitals

- residential or nursing homes

- isolated areas

- living by self or with relatives.

Abuse can happen anywhere!

Are any of the people you support vulnerable to abuse?   Yes/No

If you have answered 'Yes', please fill in the table.

Type of abuse	What can you do to prevent it happening?
1.	
2.	
3.	
4.	

  Are any of the people you support vulnerable to abuse?   Yes/No

If you have answered 'Yes', please fill in the table.

Providing Opportunities to Share Concerns

It is very unlikely that a service user will come to you and say 'I have been abused.' Therefore you will need to use your newly gained knowledge of the signs and symptoms of abuse to ascertain if anything is wrong.

> Tools need to be put in place for the people you support to tell you or others of their concerns. The workbook **Effective Communication** will give you lots of ideas.

You need to be able to communicate with the people you support and build a trusting and respectful relationship which makes the service users feel valued and respected. The service users need to communicate with you and trust you. If they do not trust you, then it is unlikely that they will confide in you. They also need to know that you will act professionally and take their concerns seriously.

You need to provide opportunities and time for the people you support to communicate with you; this can be about anything, e.g. listening to their views and preferences or things that are worrying them.

Service users need to have a copy of the complaints procedure in a format that they can understand so they can express their feelings and concerns and stop what is happening.

> Ignoring abuse is not an option.
>
> You must not prevent a person from expressing his concerns.

Reporting and Responding to Concerns

REPORTING CONCERNS

It is important that you report concerns immediately for the following reasons:

- Abuse is a criminal act.

- If you do not report your concerns, the abuse could continue and could get worse.

- You need to ensure that the service user is protected.

- You have to fulfil your duty of care.

- As an employee you need to meet the GSCC Codes of Practice, Care Standards and your local policy.

RESPONDING TO CONCERNS: WHAT TO DO!

All staff have a duty of care (protect from harm) and a responsibility to report concerns of alleged or actual abuse. You must report all factual evidence. If staff are reporting their feelings then it should be made clear that these are feelings and not facts.

You will need to:

- stay calm and offer reassurance

- be patient

- listen carefully

- show sympathy and concern

- believe what you are being told.

You will need to make notes of your concerns as soon as you can. Include where you were, details of what was said, time, date, names of people etc. Written notes are very important as they cannot be altered. You should not use whiting out fluid, because it can be said that evidence has been tampered with and will be invalid. If you make a mistake, put a line through it and initial it.

Explain what you are going to do next: you must pass this information on even though it is confidential.

Inform your manager as soon as you can. If your manager is the alleged abuser then inform his or her manager.

You should arrange for medical help if needed: you will need to tell the doctor or nurse what has happened if the service user is unable to.

Remember confidentiality and seek support for the service user and yourself.

RESPONDING TO CONCERNS: WHAT NOT TO DO!

The following is a list of what you should *not* do:

- Form your own judgement on whether disclosure is genuine.

- Wait and make sure it has happened before reporting it.

- Do nothing or keep it to yourself.

- Be afraid of expressing your concerns.

- Assume it is someone else's responsibility to report suspicions of abuse.

- Ask leading questions.

- Appear shocked, angry or disgusted.

- Promise to keep the secret or say nothing.

- Confront the alleged person.

- Tell others who do not need to know.

- Contaminate the evidence, e.g. if it is rape please discourage the service user from having a shower and washing his clothes.

- Remove the evidence, e.g. if you found a bag with child pornography in it, leave the bag there, lock the door and inform your manager. Please do not take the evidence with you.

- Make decisions on your own.

Q: Would I have to do anything different if it was a child being abused?

A: The laws that govern children are enshrined in the Children Acts 1989 and 2004. If you are supporting children, your manager will arrange for you to receive child protection training. You will also have a policy in place which tells you what you should do.

Please look at this policy if you are supporting children.

Q: What if the alleged abuser is a member of staff who is on duty at the moment? Can I send the staff member home?

A: Within your role as a social care worker, you do not have the authority to do this. You do need to safeguard the service user and you may wish to ask the service user to go with you to inform the manager of what has happened.

POLICIES

Organizations have many policies and will have either or both of these:

- policy on what to do if you suspect abuse

- policy on whistleblowing.

The whistleblowing policy provides guidance on what to do if your manager is the alleged abuser or if your manager is not acting on the information you gave.

Have you got a policy on what to do if you suspect abuse?   Yes/No

If you have answered 'Yes', please read it and answer this question:
What does the policy say you must do if you suspect abuse?

. . . .

. . . .

. . . .

. . . .

Have you got a policy titled 'Whistleblowing'?   Yes/No

If you have answered 'Yes', please read it and answer this question:

What does the policy say you must do if you suspect abuse?

. . . .

. . . .

. . . .

. . . .

Ask your manager if there is a specific form you should complete if or when you have concerns.

If you need more information you could:

- do a search on the Internet

- contact your social services department

- visit the library and read books.

CONFIDENTIALITY

Some staff may not understand what confidentiality means and therefore may not report concerns because it is confidential to the service user.

 Please now discuss with your manager what the meaning of confidentiality is and write your understanding of it here:

. . . .

. . . .

. . . .

. . . .

> Remember: do not try to investigate the matter yourself.
> You could ruin an investigation if you do!

Q: What if I am afraid to pass this information on?

A: You may find it difficult to pass on information, especially if it is about a member of the team that you know well. However, it is your duty to report any concerns. If you do not pass the concerns on, then you are as guilty as the person who is doing the abuse.

Barriers to Reporting Concerns

Service users might:

- not know the difference between abuse and good practice

- not be able to communicate in a way that staff can understand

- feel it is their fault

- feel embarrassed

- feel that they will not be believed

- be too ill to say what is happening

- think that no one can stop it happening

- not have staff around to tell (some service users live by themselves)

- be concerned about backlash from staff

- have been threatened and told not to say anything.

> If the alleged abuser is always around or on duty, it will be difficult for the service user to raise concerns. You will need to listen carefully, observe unnatural or different behaviour and pick up on any clues that something has happened.

The service user may not feel comfortable telling you what has happened. Is there a telephone that the service user can use in private to ring a relative or a friend, or CQC?   Yes/No

✍ If you have answered 'No', please discuss with your manager what can be done about this and write your answer here:

. . . .

. . . .

. . . .

. . . .

Q: If I feel I cannot speak to my manager, is there someone else I can report to?

A: Yes. The Care Quality Commission (CQC). You will find their web address at the back of this workbook. Once you are in the website, you will see a telephone number, address and email address. You do not need to give them your details: you can make a complaint anonymously.

Self-harm

 Ask your manager if you will be supporting people who self-harm in your place of work. If you are it will be written in the care plan how to provide support to the service user.

> The term self harm includes many behaviours, including cutting, burning, scalding, banging, or scratching your own body; breaking bones; pulling hair; and ingesting toxic substances or objects. The practice is often dismissed as a cry for help, a primitive method of attention seeking. However… most cases of self harm are hidden, particularly from friends and family.
>
> Chris Holley stated at a Royal College of Nursing conference in April 2006, 'It's about people who self injure in order to manage their feelings and live rather than die.' These coping strategies give a temporary fix for people who see no other way of managing emotional distress. For many people self harm is a private activity that they do not want to discuss with anyone.
>
> (Kinmond and Kinmond 2006)

What are your views on Chris Holley's statements?

. . . .

. . . .

. . . .

. . . .

> You may be supporting people who self-harm in your place of work and it is important that you provide the correct support for each individual.

✎ Please complete the following with your supervisor or manager (to ensure service users' rights to confidentiality, please do not write their names).

Have you experience of supporting people who self-harm? Yes / No

Who self-harms in your place of work? (Discuss with your supervisor but do not write the names.)

✎ In what ways do the service users self-harm?

. . . .

. . . .

✎ Why do the service users self-harm?

. . . .

. . . .

✎ What can you do to help?

. . . .

. . . .

✎ How could you make it worse?

. . . .

. . . .

✍ What effect does a person self-harming have on the people he lives with, his family, friends, other service users or the staff team?

. . . .

. . . .

. . . .

. . . .

PROTECTING FROM HARM

✍ One of the service users slips in the bath. What do you do, including any forms that you need to complete?

. . . .

. . . .

. . . .

. . . .

✍ A member of staff throws away some toiletries that belong to a service user. She says she did it because the service user is allergic to some of the contents. What do you do, including any forms that you need to complete?

. . . .

. . . .

. . . .

. . . .

Please discuss your answers with your supervisor or manager.

GOVERNMENT INQUIRIES

There are two important reports on investigations into poor practice that you may wish to read.

Investigation into the service for people with learning disabilities provided by Sutton and Merton Primary Care Trust (Commission for Healthcare Audit and Inspection 2007). Available at www.voice.org.uk/sutton.htm

Joint investigation into provision of services for people with learning disabilities at Cornwall Partnership NHS Trust (Commission for Healthcare Audit and Inspection 2006). Available at www.healthcarecommission.org.uk/_documents/cornwall_investigations_report.pdf

Questions to Test your Knowledge

✍ What is an abuser?

....

....

✍ Who can be an abuser?

....

....

✍ What is physical abuse?

....

....

✍ List two signs and symptoms of physical abuse:

1. ....

....

2. ....

....

✎ What is financial or material abuse?

. . . .

. . . .

. . . .

. . . .

✎ List two signs and symptoms of financial or material abuse:

1.　　. . . . .

. . . .

2.　　. . . . .

. . . .

✎ What is sexual abuse?

. . . .

. . . .

. . . .

. . . .

✎ List two signs and symptoms of sexual abuse:

1.　　. . . . .

. . . .

2. . . . .

. . . .

✍ What is psychological and emotional abuse?

. . . .

. . . .

. . . .

. . . .

✍ List two signs and symptoms of psychological and emotional abuse:

1. . . . .

. . . .

2. . . . .

. . . .

✍ What is neglect?

. . . .

. . . .

. . . .

. . . .

✍ List two signs and symptoms of neglect:

1. ....

....

2. ....

....

✍ What is self-neglect?

....

....

....

....

✍ List two signs and symbols of self-neglect:

1. ....

....

2. ....

....

✍ What is discriminatory abuse?

....

....

....

....

✍ List two signs and symptoms of discriminatory abuse:

1. . . . .

. . . .

2. . . . .

. . . .

✍ What is institutional abuse?

. . . .

. . . .

. . . .

. . . .

✍ List two signs and symptoms of institutional abuse:

1. . . . .

. . . .

2. . . . .

. . . .

✍ How do you know if a service user has the capacity to make a decision?

. . . .

. . . .

. . . .

. . . .

✍ Give some examples of the circumstances in which abuse might occur:

. . . .

. . . .

. . . .

. . . .

✍ Why and how does abuse 'creep' into residential homes where paid staff work?

. . . .

. . . .

. . . .

. . . .

✍ Abuse can be deliberate and intended: sometimes the wrong people become staff. Some staff may want to exert their power or control over service users. Why is this?

. . . .

. . . .

. . . .

. . . .

✍ What should you do if a service user says to you 'Don't tell anyone but...'

. . . .

. . . .

. . . .

. . . .

True and False Exercises

Try the 'true and false' exercises and check the answers with your manager.

When responding to disclosure you should:

Not ask leading questions	True/False
Be the judge and jury	True/False
Ask the service user to tell the alleged abuser what he/she has done	Truc/False
Appear shocked, angry, disgusted	True/False
Not promise to keep the secret or say nothing	True/False
Move the evidence	True/False
Confront the alleged abuser	True/False
Not tell others (who do not need to know)	True/False
Stay calm and offer reassurance	Truc/False
Not have to listen carefully and be patient	True/False
Show sympathy and concern	True/False
Explain what you are going to do next (i.e. you must pass this information on)	True/False
Arrange for medical help if needed	True/False
Institutional abuse can occur when standards and practices fall below an acceptable level	True/False

What one thing will you do differently as a result of completing this training?

. . . .

. . . .

. . . .

. . . .

Self-Assessment Tool

✍ I now know:

Who a vulnerable adult is	Yes/No
What abuse is	Yes/No
Who can be an abuser	Yes/No
What physical abuse is and its signs and symptoms	Yes/No
What financial or material abuse is and the signs and symptoms	Yes/No
What sexual abuse is and its signs and symptoms	Yes/No
What psychological and emotional abuse is and its signs and symptoms	Yes/No
What neglect is and its signs and symptoms	Yes/No
What discriminatory abuse is and its signs and symptoms	Yes/No
What institutional abuse is and its signs and symptoms	Yes/No
Circumstances when abuse may occur	Yes/No
What my organizational policy tells me to do if I suspect abuse	Yes/No
How to report and respond to concerns	Yes/No
What barriers to reporting concerns are	Yes/No

Signature of learner . . . . Date . . . .

Signature of supervisor . . . . Date . . . .

When you have completed this self-assessment tool, please do not worry if you have answered 'No' to any of the questions as you can go back and read the relevant sections again.

Certificate

. . . .

Name of company

THIS IS TO CERTIFY THAT

. . . .

Name of learner

Has completed training on

Safeguarding Adults

ON

. . . .

Date

Name of Manager/Trainer . . . .

Signature of Manager/Trainer . . . .

Name of workplace/training venue . . . .

Date . . . .

✔

This is to be written on the back of the certificate:

This training has covered:

- Prevention and protection
- Mental Capacity Act 2005
- Vulnerable adult
- Abuse
- Factors that may make abuse more likely to occur
- Different types of abuse
- The signs and symptoms of:
    - physical abuse
    - financial or material abuse
    - sexual abuse
    - psychological and emotional abuse
    - neglect
    - self-neglect
    - discriminatory abuse
    - institutional abuse
- Circumstances where abuse can occur
- Providing opportunities to share concerns
- Reporting and responding to concerns
- Barriers to reporting concerns
- Self-harm.

Knowledge Specification Chart

WHERE TO FIND THE KNOWLEDGE SPECIFICATION (KS) FOR NVQ UNIT 35

KS		Pages
1	Legal and organizational requirements on equality, diversity, discrimination, rights, confidentiality and sharing of information.	10, 14, 17, 19, 24, 26, 40, 50, 51, 73
2	How to provide active support and place the preferences and best interest of individuals at the centre of everything you do.	12, 17, 19, 24, 48
3	Dilemmas between:	
	(a) individuals' rights and their responsibilities for their own care and protection, the rights and responsibilities of key people and your role and responsibilities for their care and protection	12, 19, 20, 53, 56
	(b) individuals' views, preferences and expectations and how these can and are being met	12, 17, 18, 19, 20
	(c) your own values and those of individuals and key people	12, 18, 19, 22
	(d) your own professional values and those of others within and outside of your organizations.	12, 18, 19, 22
4	How to work in partnership with individuals, key people and those within and outside your organization to enable the individuals' needs, wishes and preferences to be met.	12, 17, 19, 48

5	Methods that are effective: (a) in promoting equality and diversity	12, 14, 17, 19, 43
	(b) when dealing with and challenging discrimination.	16, 20, 24, 25, 48
6	Codes of practice and conduct; standards and guidance relevant to your own and others' roles, responsibilities, accountability and duties for valuing and respecting individuals and key people, taking account of their views and preferences and protecting them from danger, harm and abuse.	9, 10, 14, 19, 24, 48, 50
7	Current local, UK and European legislation and organizational requirements, procedures and practices for:	
	(a) data protection, including recording, reporting, storage, security and sharing of information	12, 15, 19, 54, 56, 74
	(b) health and safety	12, 14, 39, 56, 73
	(c) risk assessment and management	12, 14, 39, 56, 73
	(d) dealing with comments and complaints	14, 47, 53
	(e) health and safety	12, 14, 39, 56, 73
	(f) the protection of yourself, individuals, key people and others from danger, harm and abuse	12, 13, 14, 15, 25, 39, 53, 56
	(g) working with others to provide integrated services.	12, 18
8	Practice and service standards relevant to your work setting and relating to valuing and respecting individuals and key people, taking account of their views and preferences and protecting them from danger, harm and abuse.	13, 14, 19, 53, 56
9	How to access records and information on the needs, views and preferences of individuals and key people.	12, 54, 73
10	The purpose of and arrangements for your supervision and appraisal.	14
11	How and where to access information and support that can inform your practice relating to valuing and respecting people, taking account of their views and preferences and protecting them from danger, harm and abuse.	12, 13, 15, 73

12	Theories relevant to the individuals with whom you work, about:	
	(a) human growth and development	17, 19
	(b) identity and self-esteem	17, 18, 19, 20, 21, 37
	(c) loss and change	20, 41
	(d) power and how it can be used and abused.	29, 32, 43
13	The effects of stress and distress.	23
14	Role of relationships and support networks in promoting the well-being of individuals.	17, 18, 28
15	Factors that affect the health, well-being, behaviour, skills, abilities and development of individuals and key people with whom you work.	12, 17, 28, 29, 35
16	Methods of supporting individuals to:	
	(a) express their needs and preferences	16, 17, 25
	(b) understand and take responsibility for promoting their own health and care	12, 57
	(c) identify how their care needs should be met	12, 57
	(d) assess and manage risks to their health and well-being.	12, 57
17	Factors that may lead to danger, harm and abuse.	25, 29
18	How to protect yourself, individuals, key people and others with whom you work from danger, harm and abuse.	12, 16, 25, 47, 48, 53
19	Signs and symptoms of danger, harm and abuse.	30
20	Correct actions to take when you suspect danger, harm and abuse or where it has been disclosed.	48, 53
21	The types of evidence that are valid in investigations and court, actions and statements that could contaminate the use of evidence.	48, 49
22	Methods that are effective in forming, maintaining and ending relationships with individuals and key people.	17, 19, 28
23	Different ways of communicating with individuals, families, carers, groups and communities about choice, well-being and protection.	16, 47

Legislation and Useful Websites

LEGISLATION THAT COULD BE APPLICABLE TO THE PEOPLE YOU SUPPORT

Care Standards Act 2000

Care Standards Act 2000 (CSA) provides for the administration of a variety of care institutions, including children's homes, independent hospitals, nursing home and residential care homes.

Data Protection Act 1998

This Act protects the rights of the individual on information that is obtained, stored, processed or supplied and applies to both computerized and paper records and requires that appropriate security measures are in place.

Human Rights Act 2000

This Act promotes the fundamental rights and freedoms contained in the European Convention on Human Rights.

Mental Capacity Act 2005

This Act provides a clearer legal framework for people who lack capacity and sets out key principles and safeguards. It also includes the 'Deprivation of liberty safeguards' which aims to provide legal protection for vulnerable people who are deprived of their liberty other than under the Mental Health Act 1983. It is planned to come into effect in April 2009.

Mental Health Act 1983

This Act regulates the treatment of mentally ill people.

NHS and Community Care Act 1990

This Act helps people live safely in the community.

Safeguarding Vulnerable Groups Act 2006

The aim of this Act is to strengthen current safeguarding arrangements and prevent unsuitable people from working with children and adults who are vulnerable. It will change the way vetting happens and will be introduced gradually from autumn 2008.

Sexual Offences Act 2003

This Act makes new provision about sexual offences, their prevention and the protection of children from harm and sexual acts.

USEFUL WEBSITES

All the following websites were accessed on 19 October 2008.

Action on Elder Abuse

www.elderabuse.org.uk

Works to protect, and prevent the abuse of, vulnerable older adults.

Age Concern

www.ageconcern.org.uk

Promotes the well-being of all older people.

Alzheimer's Society

www.alzheimers.org.uk

Leading the fight against dementia.

Care Quality Commission

www.cqc.org.uk

CQC inspect and report on care services and councils. They are independent but set up by government to improve social care and stamp out bad practice.

Communication Matters

www.communicationmatters.org.uk

Provides information in accessible formats, making information easier to understand.

Department of Health

www.dh.gov.uk

Provides health and social care policy, guidance and publications for NHS and social care professionals.

General Social Care Council

www.gscc.org.uk

Sets standards of conduct and practice for social care workers and their employers in England.

Mencap

www.mencap.org.uk

Mencap is the voice of learning disability and works with people with a learning disability to change laws and services, challenge prejudice and directly support thousands of people to live their lives as they choose.

Mind

www.mind.org.uk

Mind is the leading mental health charity in England and Wales which works to create a better life for everyone with experience of mental distress.

Respect

www.respect.uk.net

Respect is the UK membership association for domestic violence perpetrator programmes and associated support services. Their key focus is on increasing the safety of those experiencing domestic violence through promoting effective interventions with perpetrators.

Respond

www.respond.org.uk

Respond provides a range of services to both victims and perpetrators of sexual abuse who have learning disabilities and those who have been affected by other trauma. Their services extend to support and training for families, carers and professionals.

Royal National Institute for Deaf People

www.RNID.org.uk

Changing the world for deaf and hard of hearing people. RNID is the largest charity representing the nine million deaf and hard of hearing people in the UK.

Royal National Institute of Blind People

www.RNIB.org.uk

National UK charity providing a good range of information for blind or partially sighted people.

Scope

www.scope.org.uk

Scope is a UK disability organization whose focus is people with cerebral palsy.

Valuing People

www.valuingpeople.gov.uk

Valuing People is the government's plan for making the lives of people with learning disabilities and their families better.

Victim Support

www.victimsupport.org

Victim Support is the national charity which helps people affected by crime in England and Wales. They give free and confidential support to help people deal with what they've been through as a victims or witnesses, whether or not they report the crime to the police.

Women's Aid

www.womensaid.org.uk

Women's Aid is the key national charity working to end domestic violence against women and children. They support a network of over 500 domestic and sexual violence services across the UK.

References

Commission for Healthcare Audit and Inspection (2006) *Joint investigation into the provision of services for people with learning disabilities at Cornwall Partnership NHS Trust.* London: Healthcare Commission.

Commission for Healthcare Audit and Inspection (2007) *Joint investigation into the service for people with learning disabilities provided by Sutton and Merton Primary Care Trust.* London: Healthcare Commission.

Department of Health (2000) *Domiciliary Care: National Minimum Standards* (Care Quality Commission Communication Standard). London: Stationery Office.

Department of Health (2003) *Care Homes for Adults (18–65)* (Care Quality Commission Communication Standard). London: Stationery Office.

Department of Health and Home Office (2000) *No Secrets: Guidance on Developing and Implementing Multi-agency Policies and Procedures to Protect Vulnerable Adults from Abuse.* London: DoH and Home Office.

French, J.P.R. Jr, and Raven, B. (1960) 'The Bases of Social Power.' In D. Cartwright and A. Zander (eds) *Group Dynamics.* New York: Harper & Row.

General Social Care Council (GSCC) (2002) *Codes of Practice.* London: GSCC. Available at www.gscc.org.uk/codes, accessed on 19 October 2008.

James, D. (2008) 'Notifiable Incidents.' Personal email correspondence, 28 August 2008.

Kinmond, A.N. and Kinmond, K.S. (2006) 'Self harm.' *Student BMJ 14*, 397–440.

Lord Chancellor's Department (1997) *Who Decides? Making decisions on behalf of mentally incapacitated adults* (Cm 3803). London: The Stationery Office.

Maslow, A.H. (1943) 'A theory of human motivation.' *Psychological Review 50*, 370–396. Available at http://psychclassicsyorku.ca/Maslow/motivation.htm, accessed on 19 October 2008.